This Boo
Belongs to

Made in the USA
Coppell, TX
11 December 2024

41995921R00063